Beauty Babe

SET IN SOUL

This Journal Belongs To

_____

This Journal Is Dedicated To The Most Beautiful Girl Inside And Out. You.

Table Of Contents

How To Use This Journal

This Beauty Babe journal was created just for you. Whether you plan to become or are currently a makeup, hair, nails, and/or fashion enthusiast, this journal was created to help you keep track of everything regarding your appearance. As all beauty babes know, it's not only important to feel good but also look good. Being organized and simply knowing what works for you and what doesn't is what makes this journal a personalized writing experience.

Beauty Babe is filled with beauty tips as well as motivational quotes for the woman who always wants to look her best. It's not an easy job, but the goal is always to make it look effortless. This journal contains an area where you can list your favorite go-to salons and professionals. There is also a page tracker which we call 'Beauty Updates' that will help you to keep tabs on your next beauty appointments. It is recommended that you fill out this journal daily to get a better sense of what works for you and what doesn't. What makes this journal extra special is that there are faces you can color in with beauty products to see what would look great on you. You can also cut out the motivational quotes found in this journal and hang them on a wall to help you stay motivated as you get ready. We recommend taking pictures of your everyday makeup and style, printing them out, and taping them to that particular day. This may seem old-fashioned, but we believe nothing can replace the skill of writing, picture taking and picture printing. Looking good and feeling good play an important roll in your self-confidence. It doesn't matter if you're just getting started, trying to get back into the habit of taking care of yourself, or if you're an ultimate beauty babe .... it's your time to get organized and show yourself and the world how this woman does it.

Beauty Go-Tos

(A List Of Names And Locations)

Go To Dermatologist: _____

Go To Dentist: _____

Go To Makeup Artists:_____

Go To Nail Salon: _____

Go To Nail Tech: _____

Go To Back Up Nail Tech: _____

Go To Hair Salon: _____

Go To Hair Stylist: _____

Go To Hair Colorist: _____

Go To Hair Braider: _____

Go To Hair Cutter: _____

Go To Hair Extension Provider: _____

Go To Hair Extension Installer: _____

Go To Masseuse: _____

Go To Eye Brow Threader:_____

Go To Eye Brow Waxer: _____

Go To Laser Hair Removal Tech: _____

Beauty Go - Tos

Go To Body Waxer: _____

Go To Tanning Salon: _____

Go To Eyelash Applier: _____

Go To Lash Lifter: _____

Go To Shoemaker: _____

Go To Tailor/Seamstress: _____

Go To Drycleaner: _____

Go To Social Media Influencers For Makeup: _____

Go To Social Media Influencers For Fashion: _____

Go To Social Media Influencers For Hair: _____

Beauty Updates

My Last Dermatologist Visit:

_____

_____

My Next Dermatologist Visit Will Be:

_____

_____

My Last Dentist Visit:

_____

_____

My Next Dentist Visit Will Be:

_____

_____

My Last Chemical Peel Was:

_____

_____

Beauty Updates

The Next Chemical Peel Will Be:

_____

_____

My Last Teeth Whitening Job:

_____

_____

My Next Teeth Whitening Job Will Be:

_____

_____

The Last Time I Got My Nails Done:

_____

_____

The Next Time I Will Get My Next Done Will Be:

_____

_____

Beauty Updates

The Last Time I Dyed My Hair Was:

_____

_____

The Next Time I Will Dye My Hair Will Be:

_____

_____

My Last Relaxer/Chemical Straightening Job For My Hair Was:

_____

_____

The Next Relaxer/Chemical Straightening Job For My Hair Will Be:

_____

_____

My First Big Chop Was:

_____

_____

Beauty Updates

My Last Big Chop Was:

_____

_____

My Last Hair Cut/Trim:

_____

_____

My Next Hair Cut/Trim Will Be:

_____

_____

My Last Wax Hair Removal Treatment:

_____

_____

My Next Wax Hair Removal Treatment Will Be:

_____

_____

Beauty Updates

My Last Laser Hair Removal Treatment:

_____

_____

My Next Laser Hair Removal Treatment Will Be:

_____

_____

My Last Massage Was:

_____

_____

My Next Massage Will Be:

_____

_____

Getting To Know My Skin

Getting To Know My Skin

My Skin Is Currently:

My Everyday Skin Care Consists Of:

My Morning Skin Routine:

My Nightly Skin Routine:

My Skin Care For The Spring Consists Of:

Getting To Know My Skin

My Skin Care For The Summer Consists Of:

My Skin Care For The Fall Consists Of:

My Skin Care For The Winter Consists Of:

My Skin Glows When:

My Skin Goals Are:

Getting To Know My Skin

To Get To My Skin Goals, I Must:

Current Lotions I Use:

On My Face, I Currently Use:

On My Body, I Currently Use:

For Hyperpigmenation, I Use:

Getting To Know My Skin

Moisturizers That I Use On My Face That I Love Are:

Moisturizers That I Once Used On My Face That I Now Stay Away From:

My Favorite Eye Cream Is:

For Oily Skin On My Face, I Use:

For Oily Skin On My Face, I Stay Away From:

Getting To Know My Skin

For Dry Skin On My Face, I Use:

For Dry Skin On My Face, I Stay Away From:

For Combination Skin On My Face, I Use:

For Combination Skin On My Face, I Stay Away From:

For Dry Lips, I Currently Use:

Getting To Know My Skin

I Handle Dark Armpits By:

The Deodorant That I Use:

For Acne, I Use:

For Acne, I Stay Away From:

For Scars, I Use:

Getting To Know My Skin

For Scars, I Stay Away From:

I Get Rid Of Blackheads Quickly By:

I Treat Zits With:

I Currently Treat Stretch Marks By:

I Currently Treat Cellulite By:

Getting To Know My Skin

I Use To _____

_____

_____,

But Now I Love _____ About My Skin.

I Fight Wrinkles By:

I Get Rid Of Dark Circles By:

I Get Rid Of The Bags Found Under My Eyes By:

Getting To Know My Skin

I Stop The Itching After Shaving By:

The Body Scrubs That I Use Are:

The Best Face Mask For My Skin Is:

Age Defying Products I Love:

My Age Dyfing Skin Routine:

Getting To Know My Skin

Brands I Stay Away From For My Skin:

Homemade Skin Care Products I Use:

Ingredients That I Am Allergic To:

My Rules To Buying Skin Care Products For Myself:

Must-Haves And Must-Dos For My Skin:

Getting To Know My Skin

Surgical And Non-Surgical Treatments I Have Done On My Skin:

Surgical And Non-Surgical Treatments I Plan On Having On My Skin:

Health Conditions That Impact My Skin:

Family Secrets Passed Down To Me In Regards To Taking Care Of My Skin:

Extra Notes:

Getting To Know My Makeup Routines

Getting To Know My Makeup Routines

Items You Can Find In My Makeup Bag Right Now Are:

The Features Of My Face That I Like To Accentuate Are:

The Current Order I Apply Makeup:

I Am Able To Have My Makeup Last Long By:

The Best Primers For My Face Are:

Getting To Know My Makeup Routines

The Best Foundation Colors For My Complexion Are:

The Best Powders For My Complexion Are:

The Blush Colors I Love To Use Are:

The Bronzers I Love To Use Are:

The Concealers That I Love To Use Are:

Getting To Know My Makeup Routines

My Favorite Highlighters Are:

The Steps I Take To Create A Full Face Are:

My Current Foundation Routine Is:

My Favorite Lipsticks Are:

My Favorite Lip Liners Are:

Getting To Know My Makeup Routines

My Favorite Lip Glosses Are:

For A Matte Lip Color Look, I Love To Use:

For A Glossy Lip Color Look, I Love To Use:

My Favorite Soft Pink Colors For My Lips Are:

My Favorite Red Colors For My Lips Are:

Getting To Know My Makeup Routines

My Favorite Nude Colors For My Lips Are:

Other Colors That I Love On My Lips Are:

My Favorite Eyeshadow Palettes Are:

My Favorite Contour Palettes Are:

I Currently Achieve The Smokey Eye Look By:

Getting To Know My Makeup Routines

My Favorite Eye Makeup Look Is:

My Favorite Brand For Lashes Are:

My Favorite Mascaras Are:

During The Spring, My Makeup Look Is:

During The Summer, My Makeup Look Is:

Getting To Know My Makeup Routines

During The Fall, My Makeup Look Is:

During The Winter, My Makeup Look Is:

My Everyday Makeup Look Consists Of:

My Girls Night Out Makeup Look Consists Of:

My Date Night Makeup Look Consists Of:

Getting To Know My Makeup Routines

My Favorite Valentine's Day Makeup Look Consists Of:

My Favorite Church Makeup Look Consists Of:

My Favorite Everyday Workout Makeup Look Consists Of:

My Back To School Makeup Look Consists Of:

For A Bohemian Look, I Use:

Getting To Know My Makeup Routines

For An Easy Holiday Glam Look, I Use:

For A Very Vamp Look, I Use:

My Vacation Makeup Look Consists Of:

To Achieve A Glam Look, I Use:

To Achieve A Natural Look With Minimal Makeup, I Use:

Getting To Know My Makeup Routines

I Get My Eyebrows Shaped And Cleaned Up By Using:

The Products I Use To Add Definition To My Eyebrows Are:

My Favorite Drug Store Brands Are:

My Favorite Designer Makeup Brands Are:

I Learned To Do My Makeup From:

Getting To Know My Makeup Routines

My Favorite Eye Brushes Are:

My Favorite Lip Brushes Are:

My Favorite Brushes For Foundations Are:

My Favorite Brushes For Blushes Are:

My Favorite Beauty Blender Is:

Getting To Know My Makeup Routines

I Currently Clean My Makeup Brushes By:

If I Don't Have Any Makeup Remover, I Remove My Makeup By:

Makeup Brands That I Love That Use Natural Ingredients Are:

Products That I Stay Away From:

Products I Once Used That Worked For Me That No Longer Do:

Getting To Know My Makeup Routines

My Current Weekly Budget For Makeup:

My Current Monthly Budget For Makeup:

My Current Yearly Budget For Makeup:

To Remove My Makeup, I Use:

Beauty Brands I No Longer Support:

Getting To Know My Makeup Routines

Brands I Look Forward To Trying:

Ingredients That I Am Allergic To That Can Be Found In Makeup:

My Rules To Buying Makeup For Myself:

My Must-Do's For My Makeup:

My Must Not Dos When It Comes To Makeup:

Getting To Know My Makeup Routines

Surgical And/Or Non-Surgical Permanent Treatments For Makeup:

Surgical And/Or Non-Surgical Permanent Treatments I Plan On Getting That Will Give The Illusion That I Have Makeup On:

Family Secrets Passed Down To Me About Makeup:

Extra Notes:

Getting To Know My Nails

Getting To Know My Nails

My Nail Style Is:

I Often Cut My Nails Every:

I Typically Get My Nails Done Every:

The Current Way I Shape My Nails:

The Current Length Of My Nails:

Getting To Know My Nails

Current Colors I Love For My Nails:

The Spring Colors That I Love For My Nails:

The Summer Colors That I Love For My Nails:

The Fall Colors That I Love For My Nails:

The Winter Colors That I Love For My Nails:

Getting To Know My Nails

Current Colors I Stay Away From On My Nails:

The Designs That Work Best For Me Are:

Growth Aids I Use For My Nails:

I Strengthen My Nails By:

Medical Conditions That Affect My Nails:

Getting To Know My Nails

I Deal With Nail Biting By:

I Deal With Nail Infections By:

Tools I Use On My Nails Are:

The Drug Store Brand Colors That I Love Are:

My Family Secrets To Taking Care Of My Nails Are:

Getting To Know My Nails

High End Nail Polish Brand Colors I Love Are:

Must-Haves And Must-Dos For My Nails On My Hands And Toes Are:

Extra Notes:

Getting To Know My Hair

Getting To Know My Hair

Hair Type:

What I Love About My Hair:

My Hair Feels Best When:

My Current Mindset About My Hair Is:

I Believe My Hair Is:

Getting To Know My Hair

With My Hair, I Like To:

My Hair Goals Are:

The Next Steps For My Hair Are:

I Wash My Hair (State How Often):

I Deep Condition My Hair (State How Often):

Getting To Know My Hair

I Like To Detangle My Hair By:

I Add Volume To My Hair By:

I Get Rid Of Dandruff By:

The Best Dry Shampoo For My Hair:

The Best Edge Control For My Hair:

Getting To Know My Hair

The Best Hair Gel For My Hair:

Shampoos That My Hair Loves:

Products I CoWash With:

Leave Ins That My Hair Loves:

Protein Conditioners That My Hair Loves:

Getting To Know My Hair

Moisturizing Conditioners That My Hair Loves:

Oils I Use For Hot Oil Treatments:

Oils I Use To Seal In Moisture:

Hair Rinses And Hair Dyes That Work Best For Me:

Growth Aids I Use:

Getting To Know My Hair

I Maintain My Hair Health By:

I Take Care Of My Hair In The Winter By:

I Take Care Of My Hair In The Summer By:

I Get My Hair To Shine By:

After The Gym, I Take Care Of My Hair By:

Getting To Know My Hair

I Take Care Of My Dry Hair By:

I Take Care Of My Oily Hair By:

In It's Natural State, My Hair Looks & Feels:

Past Hairstyles That I Have Worn And Loved Are:

Hairstyles I Will Never Wear Again:

Getting To Know My Hair

My Go-To Hairstyle Is:

The Easiest Hairstyle For Me Is:

Hair Colors That Look Great On Me:

Hair Colors I Stay Away From:

Special Chemical Treatments I Do Periodically (Such As Brazilian Karatin Treatments, Relaxers, Highlights, Balayage, Ombre And Other Chemical Services):

Getting To Know My Hair

I Have My Hair Trimmed (List How Often You Trim Your Hair):

I Often Get A Hair Cut Every:

The Hair Product Brands I Stick To Are:

Every Morning, I:

Every Night, I:

Getting To Know My Hair

My Daily Hair Routine Consists Of:

Bad Hair Practices That I Will Stop Doing:

My Hair Needs:

My Past Hair Problems Were:

My Current Hair Problems Are:

Getting To Know My Hair

The Different Hair Styles That Look Best On Me Are:

Hair Accessories I Love To Use:

For My Thinning Hair, I Like To:

For My Thick Hair, I Like To:

For My Baby Hair, I Like To:

Getting To Know My Hair

For My Edges, I Like To:

Heating Tools I Use On My Hair:

I Like To Wear Protective Styles Such As:

My Homemade Hair Concoctions Are:

My Homemade Hair Concoctions Are For:

Getting To Know My Hair

Medical Conditions I Have That Affect My Hair:

Ingredients I Stay Away From In Hair Products:

Natural Hair Products I Love:

Hair Brands I Stay Away From:

Hand Me Down Secrets To Hair Care And Growth:

Getting To Know My Hair

List Of Life Changing Events That Have Changed My Hair:

Must-Haves And Must-Dos For My Hair:

Surgical And/Or Non-Surgical Treatments That I Have Done On My Scalp:

Surgical And/Or Non-Surgical Treatments That I Plan On Doing On My Scalp:

Extra Notes:

Getting To Know
My Personal Style

Getting To Know My Personal Style

My Body Type Is:

My Top Size Is:

My Pant Size Is:

My Dress Size Is:

My Bra Size Is:

Getting To Know My Personal Style

My Panty Size Is:

My Shoe Size Is:

Body Shapers I Like To Wear:

Colors I Love To Wear:

My Favorite Fragrances Are:

Getting To Know My Personal Style

I Would Describe My Signature Style To Be:

With My Personal Style, I Would Love To Explore:

My Style Evolved From:

My Birthday Style Is:

My Church Style Is:

Getting To Know My Personal Style

My Mommy Style Is:

My Hanging Out With The Girls Style Is:

My Gym Style Is:

My Date Night Style Is:

My Relaxed Style Is:

Getting To Know My Personal Style

My Spring/Summer Style Revolves Around These Colors And Looks:

My Fall/Winter Style Revolves Around These Colors And Looks:

The Number Of Jeans I Currently Own:

The Number Of Shoes I Currently Own:

The Number Of Dresses I Currently Own:

Getting To Know My Personal Style

The Number Of Handbags I Currently Own:

The Number Of Sunglasses I Currently Own:

The Type Of Tops That Look Great On Me Are:

The Type Of Pants That Look Great On Me Are:

The Type Of Jeans That Look Great On Me Are:

Getting To Know My Personal Style

The Types Of Dresses That Look Great On Me Are:

My Go To Jeans Are By:

My Go To Handbag Is:

Currently My Favorite Outfit Is:

I Look Sexy When I Wear:

Getting To Know My Personal Style

I Feel Confident When I Wear:

My Favorite Type Of Heels Are:

My Favorite Sandals Are:

My Favorite Sneakers Are:

My Favorite Boots Are:

Getting To Know My Personal Style

My Favorite Stilettos Are:

My Top Five Favorite Designers Are:

Current Designers That Best Reflect My Style:

Stores I Love To Shop At Are:

Favorite Vintage Stores:

Getting To Know My Personal Style

Bathing Suits That Look Amazing On Me Are:

Lingerie That Looks Amazing On Me Are:

I Would Like To Start Wearing:

Patterns That I Love:

Fabrics I Love To Wear:

Getting To Know My Personal Style

Fabrics I Stay Away From:

The Last Time I Cleaned Out My Closet Was:

The Next Time I Will Clean Out My Closet, I Will Like To Add:

Family Secrets, Tricks And Rules Passed Down To Me About Style:

Extra Notes:

Getting To Know My Jewelry And Other Accessories

Getting To Know My Jewelry And Other Accessories

My Birthstone Color Is:

My Jewelry Represents:

My Most Important Piece Of Jewelry That I Own Is:

I Like To Buy My Jewelry From:

The Type Of Earrings I Really Love Are:

Getting To Know My Jewelry And Other Accessories

Between Gold And Silver, I Prefer:

The Types Of Bracelets I Really Love To Wear:

What My Bracelets Mean To Me:

The Types Of Necklaces I Really Love To Wear:

What My Necklaces Mean To Me:

Getting To Know My Jewelry And Other Accessories

The Types Of Rings I Love To Wear:

What My Rings Mean To Me:

I Like To Mix And Match:

My Favorite Anklet:

My Jewelry Box Consists Of:

Getting To Know My Jewelry And Other Accessories

My Favorite Stones Are:

I Wear My Favorite Stones As:

I Take Care Of My Jewelry By:

I Like To Buy My Hats And Scarfs From:

The Number Of Sunglasses I Own:

Getting To Know My Jewelry And Other Accessories

Must-Haves And Must-Dos With My Jewelry And Accessories:

Jewelry Pieces That I Own That Have Been Handed Down To Me By Other Family Members Are:

Extra Notes:

Beauty And Style Challenges And Goals

Beauty And Style Challenges And Goals

Daily Beauty

Daily Beauty

Today's Mood: Date: Today's Fragrance:

Today's Affirmation:

My Body Feels:

Today My Skin Feels:

Today On My Skin I Used:

Today My Hair Looks And Feels:

Today's Beauty Food:

Today I Am Wearing:

My Style Today Is:

Today My Makeup Look Is:

For My MakeUp Look I Used:

I Internally Took

_____For

_____ .

Today's Compliment To Myself:

I Will Improve On:

Today I Made An Appointment For:

I Need To Purchase:

I No Longer Need To Purchase:

Today's Beauty Lesson Is:

Today's Beauty Lesson Came From:

Daily Beauty

Today's Mood: Date: Today's Fragrance:

Today's Affirmation:

My Body Feels:

Today My Skin Feels:

Today On My Skin I Used:

Today My Hair Looks And Feels:

Today's Beauty Food:

Today I Am Wearing:

My Style Today Is:

Today My Makeup Look Is:

For My MakeUp Look I Used:

I Internally Took

_____For

_____ .

Today's Compliment To Myself:

I Will Improve On:

Today I Made An Appointment For:

I Need To Purchase:

I No Longer Need To Purchase:

Today's Beauty Lesson Is:

Today's Beauty Lesson Came From:

Beauty And Style Notes

Today's Makeup And Beauty Products

Daily Beauty

Today's Mood: Date: Today's Fragrance:

Today's Affirmation:

My Body Feels:

Today My Skin Feels:

Today On My Skin I Used:

Today My Hair Looks And Feels:

Today's Beauty Food:

Today I Am Wearing:

My Style Today Is:

Today My Makeup Look Is:

For My MakeUp Look I Used:

I Internally Took

_____For

_____.

Today's Compliment To Myself:

I Will Improve On:

Today I Made An Appointment For:

I Need To Purchase:

I No Longer Need To Purchase:

Today's Beauty Lesson Is:

Today's Beauty Lesson Came From:

Daily Beauty

Today's Mood: Date: Today's Fragrance:

Today's Affirmation:

My Body Feels:

Today My Skin Feels:

Today On My Skin I Used:

Today My Hair Looks And Feels:

Today's Beauty Food:

Today I Am Wearing:

My Style Today Is:

Today My Makeup Look Is:

For My MakeUp Look I Used:

I Internally Took

_____For

_____ .

Today's Compliment To Myself:

I Will Improve On:

Today I Made An Appointment For:

I Need To Purchase:

I No Longer Need To Purchase:

Today's Beauty Lesson Is:

Today's Beauty Lesson Came From:

I AM NOT A TREND. I AM A CLASSIC.

I ONLY SPEAK ABOUT MY BLESSINGS.

Beauty And Style Notes

Daily Beauty

Today's Mood: Date: Today's Fragrance:

Today's Affirmation:

My Body Feels:

Today My Skin Feels:

Today On My Skin I Used:

Today My Hair Looks And Feels:

Today's Beauty Food:

Today I Am Wearing:

My Style Today Is:

Today My Makeup Look Is:

For My MakeUp Look I Used:

I Internally Took

_____For

_____.

Today's Compliment To Myself:

I Will Improve On:

Today I Made An Appointment For:

I Need To Purchase:

I No Longer Need To Purchase:

Today's Beauty Lesson Is:

Today's Beauty Lesson Came From:

Daily Beauty

Today's Mood: Date: Today's Fragrance:

Today's Affirmation:

My Body Feels:

Today My Skin Feels:

Today On My Skin I Used:

Today My Hair Looks And Feels:

Today's Beauty Food:

Today I Am Wearing:

My Style Today Is:

Today My Makeup Look Is:

For My MakeUp Look I Used:

I Internally Took

_____For

_____ .

Today's Compliment To Myself:

I Will Improve On:

Today I Made An Appointment For:

I Need To Purchase:

I No Longer Need To Purchase:

Today's Beauty Lesson Is:

Today's Beauty Lesson Came From:

Daily Beauty

Today's Mood: Date: Today's Fragrance:

Today's Affirmation:

My Body Feels:

Today My Skin Feels:

Today On My Skin I Used:

Today My Hair Looks And Feels:

Today's Beauty Food:

Today I Am Wearing:

My Style Today Is:

Today My Makeup Look Is:

For My MakeUp Look I Used:

I Internally Took

_____For

_____.

Today's Compliment To Myself:

I Will Improve On:

Today I Made An Appointment For:

I Need To Purchase:

I No Longer Need To Purchase:

Today's Beauty Lesson Is:

Today's Beauty Lesson Came From:

My New Must-Haves

Daily Beauty

Today's Mood: Date: Today's Fragrance:

Today's Affirmation:

My Body Feels:

Today My Skin Feels:

Today On My Skin I Used:

Today My Hair Looks And Feels:

Today's Beauty Food:

Today I Am Wearing:

My Style Today Is:

Today My Makeup Look Is:

For My MakeUp Look I Used:

I Internally Took

_____For

_____ .

Today's Compliment To Myself:

I Will Improve On:

Today I Made An Appointment For:

I Need To Purchase:

I No Longer Need To Purchase:

Today's Beauty Lesson Is:

Today's Beauty Lesson Came From:

Daily Beauty

Today's Mood: Date: Today's Fragrance:

Today's Affirmation:

My Body Feels:

Today My Skin Feels:

Today On My Skin I Used:

Today My Hair Looks And Feels:

Today's Beauty Food:

Today I Am Wearing:

My Style Today Is:

Today My Makeup Look Is:

For My MakeUp Look I Used:

I Internally Took

_____For

_____ .

Today's Compliment To Myself:

I Will Improve On:

Today I Made An Appointment For:

I Need To Purchase:

I No Longer Need To Purchase:

Today's Beauty Lesson Is:

Today's Beauty Lesson Came From:

Today's Makeup Slay

Beauty And Style Notes

Daily Beauty

Today's Mood: Date: Today's Fragrance:

Today's Affirmation:

My Body Feels:

Today My Skin Feels:

Today On My Skin I Used:

Today My Hair Looks And Feels:

Today's Beauty Food:

Today I Am Wearing:

My Style Today Is:

Today My Makeup Look Is:

For My MakeUp Look I Used:

I Internally Took

_____For

_____ .

Today's Compliment To Myself:

I Will Improve On:

Today I Made An Appointment For:

I Need To Purchase:

I No Longer Need To Purchase:

Today's Beauty Lesson Is:

Today's Beauty Lesson Came From:

Daily Beauty

Today's Mood: Date: Today's Fragrance:

Today's Affirmation:

My Body Feels:

Today My Skin Feels:

Today On My Skin I Used:

Today My Hair Looks And Feels:

Today's Beauty Food:

Today I Am Wearing:

My Style Today Is:

Today My Makeup Look Is:

For My MakeUp Look I Used:

I Internally Took

_____For

_____ .

Today's Compliment To Myself:

I Will Improve On:

Today I Made An Appointment For:

I Need To Purchase:

I No Longer Need To Purchase:

Today's Beauty Lesson Is:

Today's Beauty Lesson Came From:

I Have Been Spoiling Myself By

I Have Finally Accepted My

Daily Beauty

Today's Mood: Date: Today's Fragrance:

Today's Affirmation:

My Body Feels:

Today My Skin Feels:

Today On My Skin I Used:

Today My Hair Looks And Feels:

Today's Beauty Food:

Today I Am Wearing:

My Style Today Is:

Today My Makeup Look Is:

For My MakeUp Look I Used:

I Internally Took

_____For

_____ .

Today's Compliment To Myself:

I Will Improve On:

Today I Made An Appointment For:

I Need To Purchase:

I No Longer Need To Purchase:

Today's Beauty Lesson Is:

Today's Beauty Lesson Came From:

Daily Beauty

Today's Mood: Date: Today's Fragrance:

Today's Affirmation:

My Body Feels:

Today My Skin Feels:

Today On My Skin I Used:

Today My Hair Looks And Feels:

I Internally Took

_____For

_____ .

Today's Compliment To Myself:

I Will Improve On:

Today I Made An Appointment For:

Today's Beauty Food:

Today I Am Wearing:

My Style Today Is:

Today My Makeup Look Is:

For My MakeUp Look I Used:

I Need To Purchase:

I No Longer Need To Purchase:

Today's Beauty Lesson Is:

Today's Beauty Lesson Came From:

Today's Makeup And Beauty Products

Beauty And Style Notes

Daily Beauty

Today's Mood: Date: Today's Fragrance:

Today's Affirmation:

My Body Feels:

Today My Skin Feels:

Today On My Skin I Used:

Today My Hair Looks And Feels:

Today's Beauty Food:

Today I Am Wearing:

My Style Today Is:

Today My Makeup Look Is:

For My MakeUp Look I Used:

I Internally Took

_____For

_____ .

Today's Compliment To Myself:

I Will Improve On:

Today I Made An Appointment For:

I Need To Purchase:

I No Longer Need To Purchase:

Today's Beauty Lesson Is:

Today's Beauty Lesson Came From:

Daily Beauty

Today's Mood: Date: Today's Fragrance:

Today's Affirmation:

My Body Feels:

Today My Skin Feels:

Today On My Skin I Used:

Today My Hair Looks And Feels:

Today's Beauty Food:

Today I Am Wearing:

My Style Today Is:

Today My Makeup Look Is:

For My MakeUp Look I Used:

I Internally Took

_____For

_____ .

Today's Compliment To Myself:

I Will Improve On:

Today I Made An Appointment For:

I Need To Purchase:

I No Longer Need To Purchase:

Today's Beauty Lesson Is:

Today's Beauty Lesson Came From:

JUST LIKE A DIAMOND, I AM PRECIOUS AND RARE.

Daily Beauty

Today's Mood: Date: Today's Fragrance:

Today's Affirmation:

My Body Feels:

Today My Skin Feels:

Today On My Skin I Used:

Today My Hair Looks And Feels:

Today's Beauty Food:

Today I Am Wearing:

My Style Today Is:

Today My Makeup Look Is:

For My MakeUp Look I Used:

I Internally Took

_____For

_____ .

Today's Compliment To Myself:

I Will Improve On:

Today I Made An Appointment For:

I Need To Purchase:

I No Longer Need To Purchase:

Today's Beauty Lesson Is:

Today's Beauty Lesson Came From:

Today's Makeup Slay

Next Season I Plan On Changing Up My Look By

Daily Beauty

Today's Mood: Date: Today's Fragrance:

Today's Affirmation:

My Body Feels:

Today My Skin Feels:

Today On My Skin I Used:

Today My Hair Looks And Feels:

Today's Beauty Food:

Today I Am Wearing:

My Style Today Is:

Today My Makeup Look Is:

For My MakeUp Look I Used:

I Internally Took

_____For

_____ .

Today's Compliment To Myself:

I Will Improve On:

Today I Made An Appointment For:

I Need To Purchase:

I No Longer Need To Purchase:

Today's Beauty Lesson Is:

Today's Beauty Lesson Came From:

Daily Beauty

Today's Mood: Date: Today's Fragrance:

Today's Affirmation:

My Body Feels:

Today My Skin Feels:

Today On My Skin I Used:

Today My Hair Looks And Feels:

Today's Beauty Food:

Today I Am Wearing:

My Style Today Is:

Today My Makeup Look Is:

For My MakeUp Look I Used:

I Internally Took

_____For

_____ .

Today's Compliment To Myself:

I Will Improve On:

Today I Made An Appointment For:

I Need To Purchase:

I No Longer Need To Purchase:

Today's Beauty Lesson Is:

Today's Beauty Lesson Came From:

117

Daily Beauty

Today's Mood: Date: Today's Fragrance:

Today's Affirmation:

My Body Feels:

Today My Skin Feels:

Today On My Skin I Used:

Today My Hair Looks And Feels:

Today's Beauty Food:

Today I Am Wearing:

My Style Today Is:

Today My Makeup Look Is:

For My MakeUp Look I Used:

I Internally Took

_____For

_____ .

Today's Compliment To Myself:

I Will Improve On:

Today I Made An Appointment For:

I Need To Purchase:

I No Longer Need To Purchase:

Today's Beauty Lesson Is:

Today's Beauty Lesson Came From:

Today's Makeup Slay

Daily Beauty

Today's Mood: Date: Today's Fragrance:

Today's Affirmation:

My Body Feels:

Today My Skin Feels:

Today On My Skin I Used:

Today My Hair Looks And Feels:

Today's Beauty Food:

Today I Am Wearing:

My Style Today Is:

Today My Makeup Look Is:

For My MakeUp Look I Used:

I Internally Took

_____For

_____ .

Today's Compliment To Myself:

I Will Improve On:

Today I Made An Appointment For:

I Need To Purchase:

I No Longer Need To Purchase:

Today's Beauty Lesson Is:

Today's Beauty Lesson Came From:

Daily Beauty

Today's Mood: Date: Today's Fragrance:

Today's Affirmation:

My Body Feels:

Today My Skin Feels:

Today On My Skin I Used:

Today My Hair Looks And Feels:

Today's Beauty Food:

Today I Am Wearing:

My Style Today Is:

Today My Makeup Look Is:

For My MakeUp Look I Used:

I Internally Took

_____For

_____ .

Today's Compliment To Myself:

I Will Improve On:

Today I Made An Appointment For:

I Need To Purchase:

I No Longer Need To Purchase:

Today's Beauty Lesson Is:

Today's Beauty Lesson Came From:

Daily Beauty

Today's Mood: Date: Today's Fragrance:

Today's Affirmation:

My Body Feels:

Today My Skin Feels:

Today On My Skin I Used:

Today My Hair Looks And Feels:

Today's Beauty Food:

Today I Am Wearing:

My Style Today Is:

Today My Makeup Look Is:

For My MakeUp Look I Used:

I Internally Took

_____For

_____ .

Today's Compliment To Myself:

I Will Improve On:

Today I Made An Appointment For:

I Need To Purchase:

I No Longer Need To Purchase:

Today's Beauty Lesson Is:

Today's Beauty Lesson Came From:

I Have Chosen To Improve

Daily Beauty

Today's Mood: Date: Today's Fragrance:

Today's Affirmation:

My Body Feels:

Today My Skin Feels:

Today On My Skin I Used:

Today My Hair Looks And Feels:

Today's Beauty Food:

Today I Am Wearing:

My Style Today Is:

Today My Makeup Look Is:

For My MakeUp Look I Used:

I Internally Took

_____For

_____ .

Today's Compliment To Myself:

I Will Improve On:

Today I Made An Appointment For:

I Need To Purchase:

I No Longer Need To Purchase:

Today's Beauty Lesson Is:

Today's Beauty Lesson Came From:

Daily Beauty

Today's Mood: Date: Today's Fragrance:

Today's Affirmation:

My Body Feels:

Today My Skin Feels:

Today On My Skin I Used:

Today My Hair Looks And Feels:

Today's Beauty Food:

Today I Am Wearing:

My Style Today Is:

Today My Makeup Look Is:

For My MakeUp Look I Used:

I Internally Took

_____For

_____ .

Today's Compliment To Myself:

I Will Improve On:

Today I Made An Appointment For:

I Need To Purchase:

I No Longer Need To Purchase:

Today's Beauty Lesson Is:

Today's Beauty Lesson Came From:

Beauty And Style Notes

Today's Makeup Slay

Daily Beauty

Today's Mood: Date: Today's Fragrance:

Today's Affirmation:

My Body Feels:

Today My Skin Feels:

Today On My Skin I Used:

Today My Hair Looks And Feels:

Today's Beauty Food:

Today I Am Wearing:

My Style Today Is:

Today My Makeup Look Is:

For My MakeUp Look I Used:

I Internally Took

_____For

_____ .

Today's Compliment To Myself:

I Will Improve On:

Today I Made An Appointment For:

I Need To Purchase:

I No Longer Need To Purchase:

Today's Beauty Lesson Is:

Today's Beauty Lesson Came From:

Daily Beauty

Today's Mood: Date: Today's Fragrance:

Today's Affirmation:

My Body Feels:

Today My Skin Feels:

Today On My Skin I Used:

Today My Hair Looks And Feels:

Today's Beauty Food:

Today I Am Wearing:

My Style Today Is:

Today My Makeup Look Is:

For My MakeUp Look I Used:

I Internally Took

_____For

_____ .

Today's Compliment To Myself:

I Will Improve On:

Today I Made An Appointment For:

I Need To Purchase:

I No Longer Need To Purchase:

Today's Beauty Lesson Is:

Today's Beauty Lesson Came From:

I Make Pride In

Daily Beauty

Today's Mood: Date: Today's Fragrance:

Today's Affirmation:

My Body Feels:

Today My Skin Feels:

Today On My Skin I Used:

Today My Hair Looks And Feels:

Today's Beauty Food:

Today I Am Wearing:

My Style Today Is:

Today My Makeup Look Is:

For My MakeUp Look I Used:

I Internally Took

_____For

_____ .

Today's Compliment To Myself:

I Will Improve On:

Today I Made An Appointment For:

I Need To Purchase:

I No Longer Need To Purchase:

Today's Beauty Lesson Is:

Today's Beauty Lesson Came From:

Daily Beauty

Today's Mood: Date: Today's Fragrance:

Today's Affirmation:

My Body Feels:

Today My Skin Feels:

Today On My Skin I Used:

Today My Hair Looks And Feels:

Today's Beauty Food:

Today I Am Wearing:

My Style Today Is:

Today My Makeup Look Is:

For My MakeUp Look I Used:

I Internally Took

_____For

_____.

Today's Compliment To Myself:

I Will Improve On:

Today I Made An Appointment For:

I Need To Purchase:

I No Longer Need To Purchase:

Today's Beauty Lesson Is:

Today's Beauty Lesson Came From:

Today's Makeup Slay

What Makes Me Sexy

Daily Beauty

Today's Mood: Date: Today's Fragrance:

Today's Affirmation:

My Body Feels:

Today My Skin Feels:

Today On My Skin I Used:

Today My Hair Looks And Feels:

Today's Beauty Food:

Today I Am Wearing:

My Style Today Is:

Today My Makeup Look Is:

For My MakeUp Look I Used:

I Internally Took

_____For

_____ .

Today's Compliment To Myself:

I Will Improve On:

Today I Made An Appointment For:

I Need To Purchase:

I No Longer Need To Purchase:

Today's Beauty Lesson Is:

Today's Beauty Lesson Came From:

Daily Beauty

Today's Mood: Date: Today's Fragrance:

Today's Affirmation:

My Body Feels:

Today My Skin Feels:

Today On My Skin I Used:

Today My Hair Looks And Feels:

Today's Beauty Food:

Today I Am Wearing:

My Style Today Is:

Today My Makeup Look Is:

For My MakeUp Look I Used:

I Internally Took

_____For

_____ .

Today's Compliment To Myself:

I Will Improve On:

Today I Made An Appointment For:

I Need To Purchase:

I No Longer Need To Purchase:

Today's Beauty Lesson Is:

Today's Beauty Lesson Came From:

Today's Makeup Slay

Daily Beauty

Today's Mood: Date: Today's Fragrance:

Today's Affirmation:

My Body Feels:

Today My Skin Feels:

Today On My Skin I Used:

Today My Hair Looks And Feels:

Today's Beauty Food:

Today I Am Wearing:

My Style Today Is:

Today My Makeup Look Is:

For My MakeUp Look I Used:

I Internally Took

_____For

_____ .

Today's Compliment To Myself:

I Will Improve On:

Today I Made An Appointment For:

I Need To Purchase:

I No Longer Need To Purchase:

Today's Beauty Lesson Is:

Today's Beauty Lesson Came From:

Daily Beauty

Today's Mood: Date: Today's Fragrance:

Today's Affirmation:

My Body Feels:

Today My Skin Feels:

Today On My Skin I Used:

Today My Hair Looks And Feels:

Today's Beauty Food:

Today I Am Wearing:

My Style Today Is:

Today My Makeup Look Is:

For My MakeUp Look I Used:

I Internally Took

_____For

_____ .

Today's Compliment To Myself:

I Will Improve On:

Today I Made An Appointment For:

I Need To Purchase:

I No Longer Need To Purchase:

Today's Beauty Lesson Is:

Today's Beauty Lesson Came From:

Daily Beauty

Today's Mood: _____   Date: _____   Today's Fragrance: _____

Today's Affirmation:

My Body Feels:

Today My Skin Feels:

Today On My Skin I Used:

Today My Hair Looks And Feels:

Today's Beauty Food:

Today I Am Wearing:

My Style Today Is:

Today My Makeup Look Is:

For My MakeUp Look I Used:

I Internally Took

_____For

_____ .

Today's Compliment To Myself:

I Will Improve On:

Today I Made An Appointment For:

I Need To Purchase:

I No Longer Need To Purchase:

Today's Beauty Lesson Is:

Today's Beauty Lesson Came From:

I Would Describe My Beauty

Today's Makeup Slay

Daily Beauty

Today's Mood: Date: Today's Fragrance:

Today's Affirmation:

My Body Feels:

Today My Skin Feels:

Today On My Skin I Used:

Today My Hair Looks And Feels:

Today's Beauty Food:

Today I Am Wearing:

My Style Today Is:

Today My Makeup Look Is:

For My MakeUp Look I Used:

I Internally Took

_____For

_____ .

Today's Compliment To Myself:

I Will Improve On:

Today I Made An Appointment For:

I Need To Purchase:

I No Longer Need To Purchase:

Today's Beauty Lesson Is:

Today's Beauty Lesson Came From:

Daily Beauty

Today's Mood: Date: Today's Fragrance:

Today's Affirmation:

My Body Feels:

Today My Skin Feels:

Today On My Skin I Used:

Today My Hair Looks And Feels:

Today's Beauty Food:

Today I Am Wearing:

My Style Today Is:

Today My Makeup Look Is:

For My MakeUp Look I Used:

I Internally Took

_____For

_____ .

Today's Compliment To Myself:

I Will Improve On:

Today I Made An Appointment For:

I Need To Purchase:

I No Longer Need To Purchase:

Today's Beauty Lesson Is:

Today's Beauty Lesson Came From:

Daily Beauty

Today's Mood: Date: Today's Fragrance:

Today's Affirmation:

My Body Feels:

Today My Skin Feels:

Today On My Skin I Used:

Today My Hair Looks And Feels:

Today's Beauty Food:

Today I Am Wearing:

My Style Today Is:

Today My Makeup Look Is:

For My MakeUp Look I Used:

I Internally Took

_____For

_____ .

Today's Compliment To Myself:

I Will Improve On:

Today I Made An Appointment For:

I Need To Purchase:

I No Longer Need To Purchase:

Today's Beauty Lesson Is:

Today's Beauty Lesson Came From:

I Am Doing A Fantastic Job....

Daily Beauty

Today's Mood:　　　　　　　Date:　　　　　　　Today's Fragrance:

Today's Affirmation:

My Body Feels:

Today My Skin Feels:

Today On My Skin I Used:

Today My Hair Looks And Feels:

Today's Beauty Food:

Today I Am Wearing:

My Style Today Is:

Today My Makeup Look Is:

For My MakeUp Look I Used:

I Internally Took

_____For

_____ .

Today's Compliment To Myself:

I Will Improve On:

Today I Made An Appointment For:

I Need To Purchase:

I No Longer Need To Purchase:

Today's Beauty Lesson Is:

Today's Beauty Lesson Came From:

Daily Beauty

Today's Mood: Date: Today's Fragrance:

Today's Affirmation:

My Body Feels:

Today My Skin Feels:

Today On My Skin I Used:

Today My Hair Looks And Feels:

Today's Beauty Food:

Today I Am Wearing:

My Style Today Is:

Today My Makeup Look Is:

For My MakeUp Look I Used:

I Internally Took

_____For

_____ .

Today's Compliment To Myself:

I Will Improve On:

Today I Made An Appointment For:

I Need To Purchase:

I No Longer Need To Purchase:

Today's Beauty Lesson Is:

Today's Beauty Lesson Came From:

Daily Beauty

Today's Mood: Date: Today's Fragrance:

Today's Affirmation:

My Body Feels:

Today My Skin Feels:

Today On My Skin I Used:

Today My Hair Looks And Feels:

Today's Beauty Food:

Today I Am Wearing:

My Style Today Is:

Today My Makeup Look Is:

For My MakeUp Look I Used:

I Internally Took

_____For

_____ .

Today's Compliment To Myself:

I Will Improve On:

Today I Made An Appointment For:

I Need To Purchase:

I No Longer Need To Purchase:

Today's Beauty Lesson Is:

Today's Beauty Lesson Came From:

My Beautiful Lips Speak Words Of

Daily Beauty

Today's Mood: Date: Today's Fragrance:

Today's Affirmation:

My Body Feels:

Today My Skin Feels:

Today On My Skin I Used:

Today My Hair Looks And Feels:

Today's Beauty Food:

Today I Am Wearing:

My Style Today Is:

Today My Makeup Look Is:

For My MakeUp Look I Used:

I Internally Took

_____For

_____ .

Today's Compliment To Myself:

I Will Improve On:

Today I Made An Appointment For:

I Need To Purchase:

I No Longer Need To Purchase:

Today's Beauty Lesson Is:

Today's Beauty Lesson Came From:

Today's Makeup Slay

I Currently Will Be Removing From My Closet

Beauty And Style Notes

Daily Beauty

Today's Mood: Date: Today's Fragrance:

Today's Affirmation:

My Body Feels:

Today My Skin Feels:

Today On My Skin I Used:

Today My Hair Looks And Feels:

Today's Beauty Food:

Today I Am Wearing:

My Style Today Is:

Today My Makeup Look Is:

For My MakeUp Look I Used:

I Internally Took

_____For

_____ .

Today's Compliment To Myself:

I Will Improve On:

Today I Made An Appointment For:

I Need To Purchase:

I No Longer Need To Purchase:

Today's Beauty Lesson Is:

Today's Beauty Lesson Came From:

Daily Beauty

Today's Mood: Date: Today's Fragrance:

Today's Affirmation:

My Body Feels:

Today My Skin Feels:

Today On My Skin I Used:

Today My Hair Looks And Feels:

Today's Beauty Food:

Today I Am Wearing:

My Style Today Is:

Today My Makeup Look Is:

For My MakeUp Look I Used:

I Internally Took

_____For

_____ .

Today's Compliment To Myself:

I Will Improve On:

Today I Made An Appointment For:

I Need To Purchase:

I No Longer Need To Purchase:

Today's Beauty Lesson Is:

Today's Beauty Lesson Came From:

Daily Beauty

Today's Mood: Date: Today's Fragrance:

Today's Affirmation:

My Body Feels:

Today My Skin Feels:

Today On My Skin I Used:

Today My Hair Looks And Feels:

Today's Beauty Food:

Today I Am Wearing:

My Style Today Is:

Today My Makeup Look Is:

For My MakeUp Look I Used:

I Internally Took

_____For

_____ .

Today's Compliment To Myself:

I Will Improve On:

Today I Made An Appointment For:

I Need To Purchase:

I No Longer Need To Purchase:

Today's Beauty Lesson Is:

Today's Beauty Lesson Came From:

Daily Beauty

Today's Mood: _____   Date: _____   Today's Fragrance: _____

Today's Affirmation:

My Body Feels:

Today My Skin Feels:

Today On My Skin I Used:

Today My Hair Looks And Feels:

Today's Beauty Food:

Today I Am Wearing:

My Style Today Is:

Today My Makeup Look Is:

For My MakeUp Look I Used:

I Internally Took

_____For

_____ .

Today's Compliment To Myself:

I Will Improve On:

Today I Made An Appointment For:

I Need To Purchase:

I No Longer Need To Purchase:

Today's Beauty Lesson Is:

Today's Beauty Lesson Came From:

When Going Shopping For A Dress, Be Sure To Wear Your Body Shaper And Heels To Get An Accurate Look Of How The Dress Would Look When You Where It Out (If You Typically Wear A Body Shaper & Heels Out).

Today's Makeup Slay

Daily Beauty

Today's Mood: Date: Today's Fragrance:

Today's Affirmation:

My Body Feels:

Today My Skin Feels:

Today On My Skin I Used:

Today My Hair Looks And Feels:

Today's Beauty Food:

Today I Am Wearing:

My Style Today Is:

Today My Makeup Look Is:

For My MakeUp Look I Used:

I Internally Took

_____For

_____ .

Today's Compliment To Myself:

I Will Improve On:

Today I Made An Appointment For:

I Need To Purchase:

I No Longer Need To Purchase:

Today's Beauty Lesson Is:

Today's Beauty Lesson Came From:

Daily Beauty

Today's Mood: Date: Today's Fragrance:

Today's Affirmation:

My Body Feels:

Today My Skin Feels:

Today On My Skin I Used:

Today My Hair Looks And Feels:

Today's Beauty Food:

Today I Am Wearing:

My Style Today Is:

Today My Makeup Look Is:

For My MakeUp Look I Used:

I Internally Took

_____For

_____ .

Today's Compliment To Myself:

I Will Improve On:

Today I Made An Appointment For:

I Need To Purchase:

I No Longer Need To Purchase:

Today's Beauty Lesson Is:

Today's Beauty Lesson Came From:

Daily Beauty

Today's Mood: Date: Today's Fragrance:

Today's Affirmation:

My Body Feels:

Today My Skin Feels:

Today On My Skin I Used:

Today My Hair Looks And Feels:

Today's Beauty Food:

Today I Am Wearing:

My Style Today Is:

Today My Makeup Look Is:

For My MakeUp Look I Used:

I Internally Took

_____ For

_____ .

Today's Compliment To Myself:

I Will Improve On:

Today I Made An Appointment For:

I Need To Purchase:

I No Longer Need To Purchase:

Today's Beauty Lesson Is:

Today's Beauty Lesson Came From:

Daily Beauty

Today's Mood: Date: Today's Fragrance:

Today's Affirmation:

My Body Feels:

Today My Skin Feels:

Today On My Skin I Used:

Today My Hair Looks And Feels:

Today's Beauty Food:

Today I Am Wearing:

My Style Today Is:

Today My Makeup Look Is:

For My MakeUp Look I Used:

I Internally Took

_____For

_____ .

Today's Compliment To Myself:

I Will Improve On:

Today I Made An Appointment For:

I Need To Purchase:

I No Longer Need To Purchase:

Today's Beauty Lesson Is:

Today's Beauty Lesson Came From:

This Upcoming Season, I Will Wear

Daily Beauty

Today's Mood: Date: Today's Fragrance:

Today's Affirmation:

My Body Feels:

Today My Skin Feels:

Today On My Skin I Used:

Today My Hair Looks And Feels:

Today's Beauty Food:

Today I Am Wearing:

My Style Today Is:

Today My Makeup Look Is:

For My MakeUp Look I Used:

I Internally Took

_____For

_____ .

Today's Compliment To Myself:

I Will Improve On:

Today I Made An Appointment For:

I Need To Purchase:

I No Longer Need To Purchase:

Today's Beauty Lesson Is:

Today's Beauty Lesson Came From:

Daily Beauty

Today's Mood: Date: Today's Fragrance:

Today's Affirmation:

My Body Feels:

Today My Skin Feels:

Today On My Skin I Used:

Today My Hair Looks And Feels:

Today's Beauty Food:

Today I Am Wearing:

My Style Today Is:

Today My Makeup Look Is:

For My MakeUp Look I Used:

I Internally Took

_____For

_____ .

Today's Compliment To Myself:

I Will Improve On:

Today I Made An Appointment For:

I Need To Purchase:

I No Longer Need To Purchase:

Today's Beauty Lesson Is:

Today's Beauty Lesson Came From:

I Am More Than Just A Pretty Face.
I Am ....

Daily Beauty

Today's Mood: Date: Today's Fragrance:

Today's Affirmation: Today's Beauty Food:

My Body Feels: Today I Am Wearing:

Today My Skin Feels: My Style Today Is:

Today On My Skin I Used: Today My Makeup Look Is:

Today My Hair Looks And Feels: For My MakeUp Look I Used:

I Internally Took   I Need To Purchase:

_____For

_____ .

Today's Compliment To Myself: I No Longer Need To Purchase:

I Will Improve On: Today's Beauty Lesson Is:

Today I Made An Appointment For: Today's Beauty Lesson Came From:

Daily Beauty

Today's Mood: Date: Today's Fragrance:

Today's Affirmation:

My Body Feels:

Today My Skin Feels:

Today On My Skin I Used:

Today My Hair Looks And Feels:

Today's Beauty Food:

Today I Am Wearing:

My Style Today Is:

Today My Makeup Look Is:

For My MakeUp Look I Used:

I Internally Took

_____For

_____ .

Today's Compliment To Myself:

I Will Improve On:

Today I Made An Appointment For:

I Need To Purchase:

I No Longer Need To Purchase:

Today's Beauty Lesson Is:

Today's Beauty Lesson Came From:

I DO ME FOR ME.

I MAY NOT BE PERFECT, BUT I'M NO LONGER WHO YOU THINK I AM.

Daily Beauty

Today's Mood: Date: Today's Fragrance:

Today's Affirmation:

My Body Feels:

Today My Skin Feels:

Today On My Skin I Used:

Today My Hair Looks And Feels:

Today's Beauty Food:

Today I Am Wearing:

My Style Today Is:

Today My Makeup Look Is:

For My MakeUp Look I Used:

I Internally Took

_____For

_____ .

Today's Compliment To Myself:

I Will Improve On:

Today I Made An Appointment For:

I Need To Purchase:

I No Longer Need To Purchase:

Today's Beauty Lesson Is:

Today's Beauty Lesson Came From:

Daily Beauty

Today's Mood: Date: Today's Fragrance:

Today's Affirmation:

My Body Feels:

Today My Skin Feels:

Today On My Skin I Used:

Today My Hair Looks And Feels:

Today's Beauty Food:

Today I Am Wearing:

My Style Today Is:

Today My Makeup Look Is:

For My MakeUp Look I Used:

I Internally Took

_____For

_____.

Today's Compliment To Myself:

I Will Improve On:

Today I Made An Appointment For:

I Need To Purchase:

I No Longer Need To Purchase:

Today's Beauty Lesson Is:

Today's Beauty Lesson Came From:

Daily Beauty

Today's Mood: Date: Today's Fragrance:

Today's Affirmation:

My Body Feels:

Today My Skin Feels:

Today On My Skin I Used:

Today My Hair Looks And Feels:

Today's Beauty Food:

Today I Am Wearing:

My Style Today Is:

Today My Makeup Look Is:

For My MakeUp Look I Used:

I Internally Took

_____For

_____ .

Today's Compliment To Myself:

I Will Improve On:

Today I Made An Appointment For:

I Need To Purchase:

I No Longer Need To Purchase:

Today's Beauty Lesson Is:

Today's Beauty Lesson Came From:

My Stretch Marks & Cellulite Are

I AM ALWAYS IN STYLE.

Daily Beauty

Today's Mood: Date: Today's Fragrance:

Today's Affirmation:

My Body Feels:

Today My Skin Feels:

Today On My Skin I Used:

Today My Hair Looks And Feels:

Today's Beauty Food:

Today I Am Wearing:

My Style Today Is:

Today My Makeup Look Is:

For My MakeUp Look I Used:

I Internally Took

_____For

_____ .

Today's Compliment To Myself:

I Will Improve On:

Today I Made An Appointment For:

I Need To Purchase:

I No Longer Need To Purchase:

Today's Beauty Lesson Is:

Today's Beauty Lesson Came From:

Daily Beauty

Today's Mood: Date: Today's Fragrance:

Today's Affirmation:

My Body Feels:

Today My Skin Feels:

Today On My Skin I Used:

Today My Hair Looks And Feels:

Today's Beauty Food:

Today I Am Wearing:

My Style Today Is:

Today My Makeup Look Is:

For My MakeUp Look I Used:

I Internally Took

_____For

_____ .

Today's Compliment To Myself:

I Will Improve On:

Today I Made An Appointment For:

I Need To Purchase:

I No Longer Need To Purchase:

Today's Beauty Lesson Is:

Today's Beauty Lesson Came From:

I WAKE UP, STAY PRAYED UP, THEN APPLY MY MAKEUP.

Daily Beauty

Today's Mood: Date: Today's Fragrance:

Today's Affirmation:

My Body Feels:

Today My Skin Feels:

Today On My Skin I Used:

Today My Hair Looks And Feels:

Today's Beauty Food:

Today I Am Wearing:

My Style Today Is:

Today My Makeup Look Is:

For My MakeUp Look I Used:

I Internally Took

_____For

_____ .

Today's Compliment To Myself:

I Will Improve On:

Today I Made An Appointment For:

I Need To Purchase:

I No Longer Need To Purchase:

Today's Beauty Lesson Is:

Today's Beauty Lesson Came From:

Don't Get Defeated By Failure. Reapply Your Red Lipstick And Try Again.

Daily Beauty

Today's Mood: Date: Today's Fragrance:

Today's Affirmation:

My Body Feels:

Today My Skin Feels:

Today On My Skin I Used:

Today My Hair Looks And Feels:

Today's Beauty Food:

Today I Am Wearing:

My Style Today Is:

Today My Makeup Look Is:

For My MakeUp Look I Used:

I Internally Took

_____For

_____ .

Today's Compliment To Myself:

I Will Improve On:

Today I Made An Appointment For:

I Need To Purchase:

I No Longer Need To Purchase:

Today's Beauty Lesson Is:

Today's Beauty Lesson Came From:

Today's Makeup And Beauty Products

Beauty And Style Notes

Daily Beauty

Today's Mood: Date: Today's Fragrance:

Today's Affirmation:

My Body Feels:

Today My Skin Feels:

Today On My Skin I Used:

Today My Hair Looks And Feels:

Today's Beauty Food:

Today I Am Wearing:

My Style Today Is:

Today My Makeup Look Is:

For My MakeUp Look I Used:

I Internally Took

_____For

_____.

Today's Compliment To Myself:

I Will Improve On:

Today I Made An Appointment For:

I Need To Purchase:

I No Longer Need To Purchase:

Today's Beauty Lesson Is:

Today's Beauty Lesson Came From:

Daily Beauty

Today's Mood: Date: Today's Fragrance:

Today's Affirmation:

My Body Feels:

Today My Skin Feels:

Today On My Skin I Used:

Today My Hair Looks And Feels:

Today's Beauty Food:

Today I Am Wearing:

My Style Today Is:

Today My Makeup Look Is:

For My MakeUp Look I Used:

I Internally Took

_____For

_____.

Today's Compliment To Myself:

I Will Improve On:

Today I Made An Appointment For:

I Need To Purchase:

I No Longer Need To Purchase:

Today's Beauty Lesson Is:

Today's Beauty Lesson Came From:

Today's Makeup Slay

A List Of Beauty Secrets I Have Learned From Important Women In My Life

Beauty And Style Notes

Daily Beauty

Today's Mood: Date: Today's Fragrance:

Today's Affirmation:

My Body Feels:

Today My Skin Feels:

Today On My Skin I Used:

Today My Hair Looks And Feels:

Today's Beauty Food:

Today I Am Wearing:

My Style Today Is:

Today My Makeup Look Is:

For My MakeUp Look I Used:

I Internally Took

_____For

_____ .

Today's Compliment To Myself:

I Will Improve On:

Today I Made An Appointment For:

I Need To Purchase:

I No Longer Need To Purchase:

Today's Beauty Lesson Is:

Today's Beauty Lesson Came From:

WHEN I LOOK AT MYSELF IN THE MIRROR, THERE IS SO MUCH TO SMILE ABOUT.

Daily Beauty

Today's Mood: Date: Today's Fragrance:

Today's Affirmation:

My Body Feels:

Today My Skin Feels:

Today On My Skin I Used:

Today My Hair Looks And Feels:

Today's Beauty Food:

Today I Am Wearing:

My Style Today Is:

Today My Makeup Look Is:

For My MakeUp Look I Used:

I Internally Took

_____For

_____ .

Today's Compliment To Myself:

I Will Improve On:

Today I Made An Appointment For:

I Need To Purchase:

I No Longer Need To Purchase:

Today's Beauty Lesson Is:

Today's Beauty Lesson Came From:

Daily Beauty

Today's Mood: Date: Today's Fragrance:

Today's Affirmation:

My Body Feels:

Today My Skin Feels:

Today On My Skin I Used:

Today My Hair Looks And Feels:

Today's Beauty Food:

Today I Am Wearing:

My Style Today Is:

Today My Makeup Look Is:

For My MakeUp Look I Used:

I Internally Took

_____For

_____ .

Today's Compliment To Myself:

I Will Improve On:

Today I Made An Appointment For:

I Need To Purchase:

I No Longer Need To Purchase:

Today's Beauty Lesson Is:

Today's Beauty Lesson Came From:

Daily Beauty

Today's Mood: Date: Today's Fragrance:

Today's Affirmation:

My Body Feels:

Today My Skin Feels:

Today On My Skin I Used:

Today My Hair Looks And Feels:

Today's Beauty Food:

Today I Am Wearing:

My Style Today Is:

Today My Makeup Look Is:

For My MakeUp Look I Used:

I Internally Took

_____For

_____ .

Today's Compliment To Myself:

I Will Improve On:

Today I Made An Appointment For:

I Need To Purchase:

I No Longer Need To Purchase:

Today's Beauty Lesson Is:

Today's Beauty Lesson Came From:

I SPARKLE EVERYDAY.

Daily Beauty

Today's Mood: Date: Today's Fragrance:

Today's Affirmation:

My Body Feels:

Today My Skin Feels:

Today On My Skin I Used:

Today My Hair Looks And Feels:

Today's Beauty Food:

Today I Am Wearing:

My Style Today Is:

Today My Makeup Look Is:

For My MakeUp Look I Used:

I Internally Took

_____For

_____ .

Today's Compliment To Myself:

I Will Improve On:

Today I Made An Appointment For:

I Need To Purchase:

I No Longer Need To Purchase:

Today's Beauty Lesson Is:

Today's Beauty Lesson Came From:

Daily Beauty

Today's Mood: Date: Today's Fragrance:

Today's Affirmation:

My Body Feels:

Today My Skin Feels:

Today On My Skin I Used:

Today My Hair Looks And Feels:

Today's Beauty Food:

Today I Am Wearing:

My Style Today Is:

Today My Makeup Look Is:

For My MakeUp Look I Used:

I Internally Took

_____For

_____.

Today's Compliment To Myself:

I Will Improve On:

Today I Made An Appointment For:

I Need To Purchase:

I No Longer Need To Purchase:

Today's Beauty Lesson Is:

Today's Beauty Lesson Came From:

I AM BEAUTIFUL BECAUSE I AM MYSELF.

Daily Beauty

Today's Mood: Date: Today's Fragrance:

Today's Affirmation:

My Body Feels:

Today My Skin Feels:

Today On My Skin I Used:

Today My Hair Looks And Feels:

Today's Beauty Food:

Today I Am Wearing:

My Style Today Is:

Today My Makeup Look Is:

For My MakeUp Look I Used:

I Internally Took

_____For

_____ .

Today's Compliment To Myself:

I Will Improve On:

Today I Made An Appointment For:

I Need To Purchase:

I No Longer Need To Purchase:

Today's Beauty Lesson Is:

Today's Beauty Lesson Came From:

Daily Beauty

Today's Mood: Date: Today's Fragrance:

Today's Affirmation: Today's Beauty Food:

My Body Feels: Today I Am Wearing:

Today My Skin Feels: My Style Today Is:

Today On My Skin I Used: Today My Makeup Look Is:

Today My Hair Looks And Feels: For My MakeUp Look I Used:

I Internally Took   I Need To Purchase:

_____For

_____ .

Today's Compliment To Myself: I No Longer Need To Purchase:

I Will Improve On: Today's Beauty Lesson Is:

Today I Made An Appointment For: Today's Beauty Lesson Came From:

Daily Beauty

Today's Mood: _____ Date: _____ Today's Fragrance: _____

Today's Affirmation:

My Body Feels:

Today My Skin Feels:

Today On My Skin I Used:

Today My Hair Looks And Feels:

Today's Beauty Food:

Today I Am Wearing:

My Style Today Is:

Today My Makeup Look Is:

For My MakeUp Look I Used:

I Internally Took

_____For

_____ .

Today's Compliment To Myself:

I Will Improve On:

Today I Made An Appointment For:

I Need To Purchase:

I No Longer Need To Purchase:

Today's Beauty Lesson Is:

Today's Beauty Lesson Came From:

Daily Beauty

Today's Mood: Date: Today's Fragrance:

Today's Affirmation:

My Body Feels:

Today My Skin Feels:

Today On My Skin I Used:

Today My Hair Looks And Feels:

Today's Beauty Food:

Today I Am Wearing:

My Style Today Is:

Today My Makeup Look Is:

For My MakeUp Look I Used:

I Internally Took

_____For

_____ .

Today's Compliment To Myself:

I Will Improve On:

Today I Made An Appointment For:

I Need To Purchase:

I No Longer Need To Purchase:

Today's Beauty Lesson Is:

Today's Beauty Lesson Came From:

I AM _____

I AM _____

I AM _____

I AM _____

I AM _____

I AM _____

I AM _____

I AM _____

Today's Makeup Slay

Beauty And Style Notes

Daily Beauty

Today's Mood: Date: Today's Fragrance:

Today's Affirmation: Today's Beauty Food:

My Body Feels: Today I Am Wearing:

Today My Skin Feels: My Style Today Is:

Today On My Skin I Used: Today My Makeup Look Is:

Today My Hair Looks And Feels: For My MakeUp Look I Used:

I Internally Took   I Need To Purchase:

_____For

_____ .

Today's Compliment To Myself: I No Longer Need To Purchase:

I Will Improve On: Today's Beauty Lesson Is:

Today I Made An Appointment For: Today's Beauty Lesson Came From:

Daily Beauty

Today's Mood: Date: Today's Fragrance:

Today's Affirmation:

My Body Feels:

Today My Skin Feels:

Today On My Skin I Used:

Today My Hair Looks And Feels:

Today's Beauty Food:

Today I Am Wearing:

My Style Today Is:

Today My Makeup Look Is:

For My MakeUp Look I Used:

I Internally Took

_____For

_____ .

Today's Compliment To Myself:

I Will Improve On:

Today I Made An Appointment For:

I Need To Purchase:

I No Longer Need To Purchase:

Today's Beauty Lesson Is:

Today's Beauty Lesson Came From:

Daily Beauty

Today's Mood: Date: Today's Fragrance:

Today's Affirmation:

My Body Feels:

Today My Skin Feels:

Today On My Skin I Used:

Today My Hair Looks And Feels:

Today's Beauty Food:

Today I Am Wearing:

My Style Today Is:

Today My Makeup Look Is:

For My MakeUp Look I Used:

I Internally Took

_____For

_____ .

Today's Compliment To Myself:

I Will Improve On:

Today I Made An Appointment For:

I Need To Purchase:

I No Longer Need To Purchase:

Today's Beauty Lesson Is:

Today's Beauty Lesson Came From:

CHARACTER. INTELLIGENCE. STYLE.

CHARACTER. INTELLIGENCE. STYLE.

CHARACTER. INTELLIGENCE. STYLE.

CHARACTER. INTELLIGENCE. STYLE.

Daily Beauty

Today's Mood: Date: Today's Fragrance:

Today's Affirmation: Today's Beauty Food:

My Body Feels: Today I Am Wearing:

Today My Skin Feels: My Style Today Is:

Today On My Skin I Used: Today My Makeup Look Is:

Today My Hair Looks And Feels: For My MakeUp Look I Used:

I Internally Took   I Need To Purchase:

_____For

_____ .

Today's Compliment To Myself: I No Longer Need To Purchase:

I Will Improve On: Today's Beauty Lesson Is:

Today I Made An Appointment For: Today's Beauty Lesson Came From:

Daily Beauty

Today's Mood: Date: Today's Fragrance:

Today's Affirmation:

My Body Feels:

Today My Skin Feels:

Today On My Skin I Used:

Today My Hair Looks And Feels:

Today's Beauty Food:

Today I Am Wearing:

My Style Today Is:

Today My Makeup Look Is:

For My MakeUp Look I Used:

I Internally Took

_____For

_____ .

Today's Compliment To Myself:

I Will Improve On:

Today I Made An Appointment For:

I Need To Purchase:

I No Longer Need To Purchase:

Today's Beauty Lesson Is:

Today's Beauty Lesson Came From:

I AM BEAUTIFUL.

I AM STRONGER THAN I SEEM.

Daily Beauty

Today's Mood: Date: Today's Fragrance:

Today's Affirmation:

My Body Feels:

Today My Skin Feels:

Today On My Skin I Used:

Today My Hair Looks And Feels:

Today's Beauty Food:

Today I Am Wearing:

My Style Today Is:

Today My Makeup Look Is:

For My MakeUp Look I Used:

I Internally Took

_____For

_____ .

Today's Compliment To Myself:

I Will Improve On:

Today I Made An Appointment For:

I Need To Purchase:

I No Longer Need To Purchase:

Today's Beauty Lesson Is:

Today's Beauty Lesson Came From:

Daily Beauty

Today's Mood: Date: Today's Fragrance:

Today's Affirmation:

My Body Feels:

Today My Skin Feels:

Today On My Skin I Used:

Today My Hair Looks And Feels:

Today's Beauty Food:

Today I Am Wearing:

My Style Today Is:

Today My Makeup Look Is:

For My MakeUp Look I Used:

I Internally Took

_____For

_____ .

Today's Compliment To Myself:

I Will Improve On:

Today I Made An Appointment For:

I Need To Purchase:

I No Longer Need To Purchase:

Today's Beauty Lesson Is:

Today's Beauty Lesson Came From:

215

Beauty And Style Notes

Daily Beauty

Today's Mood: Date: Today's Fragrance:

Today's Affirmation:

My Body Feels:

Today My Skin Feels:

Today On My Skin I Used:

Today My Hair Looks And Feels:

Today's Beauty Food:

Today I Am Wearing:

My Style Today Is:

Today My Makeup Look Is:

For My MakeUp Look I Used:

I Internally Took

_____For

_____ .

Today's Compliment To Myself:

I Will Improve On:

Today I Made An Appointment For:

I Need To Purchase:

I No Longer Need To Purchase:

Today's Beauty Lesson Is:

Today's Beauty Lesson Came From:

Daily Beauty

Today's Mood:  Date: Today's Fragrance:

Today's Affirmation:

My Body Feels:

Today My Skin Feels:

Today On My Skin I Used:

Today My Hair Looks And Feels:

Today's Beauty Food:

Today I Am Wearing:

My Style Today Is:

Today My Makeup Look Is:

For My MakeUp Look I Used:

I Internally Took

_____For

_____.

Today's Compliment To Myself:

I Will Improve On:

Today I Made An Appointment For:

I Need To Purchase:

I No Longer Need To Purchase:

Today's Beauty Lesson Is:

Today's Beauty Lesson Came From:

ANOTHER WOMAN'S BEAUTY DOES NOT DIMINISH MY OWN.

I BELIEVE IN MYSELF.

I BELIEVE IN MYSELF.

I BELIEVE IN MYSELF.

I BELIEVE IN MYSELF.

Daily Beauty

Today's Mood: Date: Today's Fragrance:

Today's Affirmation:

My Body Feels:

Today My Skin Feels:

Today On My Skin I Used:

Today My Hair Looks And Feels:

Today's Beauty Food:

Today I Am Wearing:

My Style Today Is:

Today My Makeup Look Is:

For My MakeUp Look I Used:

I Internally Took

_____For

_____.

Today's Compliment To Myself:

I Will Improve On:

Today I Made An Appointment For:

I Need To Purchase:

I No Longer Need To Purchase:

Today's Beauty Lesson Is:

Today's Beauty Lesson Came From:

Daily Beauty

Today's Mood: Date: Today's Fragrance:

Today's Affirmation:

My Body Feels:

Today My Skin Feels:

Today On My Skin I Used:

Today My Hair Looks And Feels:

Today's Beauty Food:

Today I Am Wearing:

My Style Today Is:

Today My Makeup Look Is:

For My MakeUp Look I Used:

I Internally Took

_____For

_____.

Today's Compliment To Myself:

I Will Improve On:

Today I Made An Appointment For:

I Need To Purchase:

I No Longer Need To Purchase:

Today's Beauty Lesson Is:

Today's Beauty Lesson Came From:

Treat Your Body Right And Make Time To Exercise.

223

Daily Beauty

Today's Mood: Date: Today's Fragrance:

Today's Affirmation:

My Body Feels:

Today My Skin Feels:

Today On My Skin I Used:

Today My Hair Looks And Feels:

Today's Beauty Food:

Today I Am Wearing:

My Style Today Is:

Today My Makeup Look Is:

For My MakeUp Look I Used:

I Internally Took

_____For

_____ .

Today's Compliment To Myself:

I Will Improve On:

Today I Made An Appointment For:

I Need To Purchase:

I No Longer Need To Purchase:

Today's Beauty Lesson Is:

Today's Beauty Lesson Came From:

I Feel Most Confident When I

Beauty And Style Notes

Today's Makeup Slay

Daily Beauty

Today's Mood: Date: Today's Fragrance:

Today's Affirmation:

My Body Feels:

Today My Skin Feels:

Today On My Skin I Used:

Today My Hair Looks And Feels:

Today's Beauty Food:

Today I Am Wearing:

My Style Today Is:

Today My Makeup Look Is:

For My MakeUp Look I Used:

I Internally Took

_____For

_____ .

Today's Compliment To Myself:

I Will Improve On:

Today I Made An Appointment For:

I Need To Purchase:

I No Longer Need To Purchase:

Today's Beauty Lesson Is:

Today's Beauty Lesson Came From:

Daily Beauty

Today's Mood: Date: Today's Fragrance:

Today's Affirmation:

My Body Feels:

Today My Skin Feels:

Today On My Skin I Used:

Today My Hair Looks And Feels:

Today's Beauty Food:

Today I Am Wearing:

My Style Today Is:

Today My Makeup Look Is:

For My MakeUp Look I Used:

I Internally Took

_____For

_____ .

Today's Compliment To Myself:

I Will Improve On:

Today I Made An Appointment For:

I Need To Purchase:

I No Longer Need To Purchase:

Today's Beauty Lesson Is:

Today's Beauty Lesson Came From:

I HAVE ACCEPTED WHO I AM. I LOVE MYSELF FOR THAT.

Daily Beauty

Today's Mood: _____   Date: _____   Today's Fragrance: _____

Today's Affirmation:

My Body Feels:

Today My Skin Feels:

Today On My Skin I Used:

Today My Hair Looks And Feels:

Today's Beauty Food:

Today I Am Wearing:

My Style Today Is:

Today My Makeup Look Is:

For My MakeUp Look I Used:

I Internally Took

_____For

_____.

Today's Compliment To Myself:

I Will Improve On:

Today I Made An Appointment For:

I Need To Purchase:

I No Longer Need To Purchase:

Today's Beauty Lesson Is:

Today's Beauty Lesson Came From:

Daily Beauty

Today's Mood: Date: Today's Fragrance:

Today's Affirmation:

My Body Feels:

Today My Skin Feels:

Today On My Skin I Used:

Today My Hair Looks And Feels:

Today's Beauty Food:

Today I Am Wearing:

My Style Today Is:

Today My Makeup Look Is:

For My MakeUp Look I Used:

I Internally Took

_____For

_____ .

Today's Compliment To Myself:

I Will Improve On:

Today I Made An Appointment For:

I Need To Purchase:

I No Longer Need To Purchase:

Today's Beauty Lesson Is:

Today's Beauty Lesson Came From:

Today's Makeup Slay

Daily Beauty

Today's Mood: Date: Today's Fragrance:

Today's Affirmation: Today's Beauty Food:

My Body Feels: Today I Am Wearing:

Today My Skin Feels: My Style Today Is:

Today On My Skin I Used: Today My Makeup Look Is:

Today My Hair Looks And Feels: For My MakeUp Look I Used:

I Internally Took   I Need To Purchase:

_____For

_____ .

Today's Compliment To Myself: I No Longer Need To Purchase:

I Will Improve On: Today's Beauty Lesson Is:

Today I Made An Appointment For: Today's Beauty Lesson Came From:

Never Be Afraid To Say No.

Daily Beauty

Today's Mood: Date: Today's Fragrance:

Today's Affirmation:

My Body Feels:

Today My Skin Feels:

Today On My Skin I Used:

Today My Hair Looks And Feels:

Today's Beauty Food:

Today I Am Wearing:

My Style Today Is:

Today My Makeup Look Is:

For My MakeUp Look I Used:

I Internally Took

_____ For

_____ .

Today's Compliment To Myself:

I Will Improve On:

Today I Made An Appointment For:

I Need To Purchase:

I No Longer Need To Purchase:

Today's Beauty Lesson Is:

Today's Beauty Lesson Came From:

Daily Beauty

Today's Mood: Date: Today's Fragrance:

Today's Affirmation:

My Body Feels:

Today My Skin Feels:

Today On My Skin I Used:

Today My Hair Looks And Feels:

Today's Beauty Food:

Today I Am Wearing:

My Style Today Is:

Today My Makeup Look Is:

For My MakeUp Look I Used:

I Internally Took

_____For

_____ .

Today's Compliment To Myself:

I Will Improve On:

Today I Made An Appointment For:

I Need To Purchase:

I No Longer Need To Purchase:

Today's Beauty Lesson Is:

Today's Beauty Lesson Came From:

Daily Beauty

Today's Mood: Date: Today's Fragrance:

Today's Affirmation:

My Body Feels:

Today My Skin Feels:

Today On My Skin I Used:

Today My Hair Looks And Feels:

Today's Beauty Food:

Today I Am Wearing:

My Style Today Is:

Today My Makeup Look Is:

For My MakeUp Look I Used:

I Internally Took

_____For

_____ .

Today's Compliment To Myself:

I Will Improve On:

Today I Made An Appointment For:

I Need To Purchase:

I No Longer Need To Purchase:

Today's Beauty Lesson Is:

Today's Beauty Lesson Came From:

I AM TOO PRETTY TO BE BOTHERED.

Daily Beauty

Today's Mood: Date: Today's Fragrance:

Today's Affirmation:

My Body Feels:

Today My Skin Feels:

Today On My Skin I Used:

Today My Hair Looks And Feels:

Today's Beauty Food:

Today I Am Wearing:

My Style Today Is:

Today My Makeup Look Is:

For My MakeUp Look I Used:

I Internally Took

_____For

_____ .

Today's Compliment To Myself:

I Will Improve On:

Today I Made An Appointment For:

I Need To Purchase:

I No Longer Need To Purchase:

Today's Beauty Lesson Is:

Today's Beauty Lesson Came From:

Daily Beauty

Today's Mood: Date: Today's Fragrance:

Today's Affirmation:

My Body Feels:

Today My Skin Feels:

Today On My Skin I Used:

Today My Hair Looks And Feels:

Today's Beauty Food:

Today I Am Wearing:

My Style Today Is:

Today My Makeup Look Is:

For My MakeUp Look I Used:

I Internally Took

_____For

_____ .

Today's Compliment To Myself:

I Will Improve On:

Today I Made An Appointment For:

I Need To Purchase:

I No Longer Need To Purchase:

Today's Beauty Lesson Is:

Today's Beauty Lesson Came From:

Daily Beauty

Today's Mood: _____ Date: _____ Today's Fragrance: _____

Today's Affirmation:

My Body Feels:

Today My Skin Feels:

Today On My Skin I Used:

Today My Hair Looks And Feels:

Today's Beauty Food:

Today I Am Wearing:

My Style Today Is:

Today My Makeup Look Is:

For My MakeUp Look I Used:

I Internally Took

_____For

_____ .

Today's Compliment To Myself:

I Will Improve On:

Today I Made An Appointment For:

I Need To Purchase:

I No Longer Need To Purchase:

Today's Beauty Lesson Is:

Today's Beauty Lesson Came From:

I'M NOT EVEN WHO I AM YET AND I'M STILL BEING BLESSED.

Daily Beauty

Today's Mood: Date: Today's Fragrance:

Today's Affirmation:

My Body Feels:

Today My Skin Feels:

Today On My Skin I Used:

Today My Hair Looks And Feels:

Today's Beauty Food:

Today I Am Wearing:

My Style Today Is:

Today My Makeup Look Is:

For My MakeUp Look I Used:

I Internally Took

_____For

_____ .

Today's Compliment To Myself:

I Will Improve On:

Today I Made An Appointment For:

I Need To Purchase:

I No Longer Need To Purchase:

Today's Beauty Lesson Is:

Today's Beauty Lesson Came From:

I AM BEAUTIFUL BECAUSE OF THE SPIRIT WITHIN ME.

BIG
HAIR.

BIG
HEART.

BIG
DREAMS.

Daily Beauty

Today's Mood: Date: Today's Fragrance:

Today's Affirmation:

My Body Feels:

Today My Skin Feels:

Today On My Skin I Used:

Today My Hair Looks And Feels:

Today's Beauty Food:

Today I Am Wearing:

My Style Today Is:

Today My Makeup Look Is:

For My MakeUp Look I Used:

I Internally Took

_____For

_____ .

Today's Compliment To Myself:

I Will Improve On:

Today I Made An Appointment For:

I Need To Purchase:

I No Longer Need To Purchase:

Today's Beauty Lesson Is:

Today's Beauty Lesson Came From:

Daily Beauty

Today's Mood: Date: Today's Fragrance:

Today's Affirmation:

My Body Feels:

Today My Skin Feels:

Today On My Skin I Used:

Today My Hair Looks And Feels:

Today's Beauty Food:

Today I Am Wearing:

My Style Today Is:

Today My Makeup Look Is:

For My MakeUp Look I Used:

I Internally Took

_____For

_____ .

Today's Compliment To Myself:

I Will Improve On:

Today I Made An Appointment For:

I Need To Purchase:

I No Longer Need To Purchase:

Today's Beauty Lesson Is:

Today's Beauty Lesson Came From:

Today's Makeup And Beauty Products

Today's Makeup Slay

Daily Beauty

Today's Mood: Date: Today's Fragrance:

Today's Affirmation:

My Body Feels:

Today My Skin Feels:

Today On My Skin I Used:

Today My Hair Looks And Feels:

Today's Beauty Food:

Today I Am Wearing:

My Style Today Is:

Today My Makeup Look Is:

For My MakeUp Look I Used:

I Internally Took

_____For

_____.

Today's Compliment To Myself:

I Will Improve On:

Today I Made An Appointment For:

I Need To Purchase:

I No Longer Need To Purchase:

Today's Beauty Lesson Is:

Today's Beauty Lesson Came From:

Daily Beauty

Today's Mood: Date: Today's Fragrance:

Today's Affirmation:

My Body Feels:

Today My Skin Feels:

Today On My Skin I Used:

Today My Hair Looks And Feels:

Today's Beauty Food:

Today I Am Wearing:

My Style Today Is:

Today My Makeup Look Is:

For My MakeUp Look I Used:

I Internally Took

_____For

_____ .

Today's Compliment To Myself:

I Will Improve On:

Today I Made An Appointment For:

I Need To Purchase:

I No Longer Need To Purchase:

Today's Beauty Lesson Is:

Today's Beauty Lesson Came From:

Figure Out Your Favorite Item Of Clothing And/Or Jewelry and Make That Part Of Your Signature Look.

Beauty And Style Notes

Today's Makeup Slay

TO MY HAIR,

I WILL ALWAYS LOVE YOU.

I ALSO LOVE THE PARTS OF ME THAT ISN'T COVERED BY MAKEUP.

Daily Beauty

Today's Mood: Date: Today's Fragrance:

Today's Affirmation:

My Body Feels:

Today My Skin Feels:

Today On My Skin I Used:

Today My Hair Looks And Feels:

Today's Beauty Food:

Today I Am Wearing:

My Style Today Is:

Today My Makeup Look Is:

For My MakeUp Look I Used:

I Internally Took

_____For

_____ .

Today's Compliment To Myself:

I Will Improve On:

Today I Made An Appointment For:

I Need To Purchase:

I No Longer Need To Purchase:

Today's Beauty Lesson Is:

Today's Beauty Lesson Came From:

Daily Beauty

Today's Mood: Date: Today's Fragrance:

Today's Affirmation:

My Body Feels:

Today My Skin Feels:

Today On My Skin I Used:

Today My Hair Looks And Feels:

Today's Beauty Food:

Today I Am Wearing:

My Style Today Is:

Today My Makeup Look Is:

For My MakeUp Look I Used:

I Internally Took

_____For

_____ .

Today's Compliment To Myself:

I Will Improve On:

Today I Made An Appointment For:

I Need To Purchase:

I No Longer Need To Purchase:

Today's Beauty Lesson Is:

Today's Beauty Lesson Came From:

Daily Beauty

Today's Mood: Date: Today's Fragrance:

Today's Affirmation:

My Body Feels:

Today My Skin Feels:

Today On My Skin I Used:

Today My Hair Looks And Feels:

Today's Beauty Food:

Today I Am Wearing:

My Style Today Is:

Today My Makeup Look Is:

For My MakeUp Look I Used:

I Internally Took

_____For

_____ .

Today's Compliment To Myself:

I Will Improve On:

Today I Made An Appointment For:

I Need To Purchase:

I No Longer Need To Purchase:

Today's Beauty Lesson Is:

Today's Beauty Lesson Came From:

The Next Few Items I Plan On Buying Are ....

Daily Beauty

Today's Mood: Date: Today's Fragrance:

Today's Affirmation:

My Body Feels:

Today My Skin Feels:

Today On My Skin I Used:

Today My Hair Looks And Feels:

Today's Beauty Food:

Today I Am Wearing:

My Style Today Is:

Today My Makeup Look Is:

For My MakeUp Look I Used:

I Internally Took

_____For

_____ .

Today's Compliment To Myself:

I Will Improve On:

Today I Made An Appointment For:

I Need To Purchase:

I No Longer Need To Purchase:

Today's Beauty Lesson Is:

Today's Beauty Lesson Came From:

Daily Beauty

Today's Mood: Date: Today's Fragrance:

Today's Affirmation:

My Body Feels:

Today My Skin Feels:

Today On My Skin I Used:

Today My Hair Looks And Feels:

Today's Beauty Food:

Today I Am Wearing:

My Style Today Is:

Today My Makeup Look Is:

For My MakeUp Look I Used:

I Internally Took

_____For

_____ .

Today's Compliment To Myself:

I Will Improve On:

Today I Made An Appointment For:

I Need To Purchase:

I No Longer Need To Purchase:

Today's Beauty Lesson Is:

Today's Beauty Lesson Came From:

Today's Makeup Slay

Beauty And Style Notes

Daily Beauty

Today's Mood: Date: Today's Fragrance:

Today's Affirmation:

My Body Feels:

Today My Skin Feels:

Today On My Skin I Used:

Today My Hair Looks And Feels:

Today's Beauty Food:

Today I Am Wearing:

My Style Today Is:

Today My Makeup Look Is:

For My MakeUp Look I Used:

I Internally Took

_____For

_____ .

Today's Compliment To Myself:

I Will Improve On:

Today I Made An Appointment For:

I Need To Purchase:

I No Longer Need To Purchase:

Today's Beauty Lesson Is:

Today's Beauty Lesson Came From:

Daily Beauty

Today's Mood: Date: Today's Fragrance:

Today's Affirmation: Today's Beauty Food:

My Body Feels: Today I Am Wearing:

Today My Skin Feels: My Style Today Is:

Today On My Skin I Used: Today My Makeup Look Is:

Today My Hair Looks And Feels: For My MakeUp Look I Used:

I Internally Took   I Need To Purchase:

_____For

_____.

Today's Compliment To Myself: I No Longer Need To Purchase:

I Will Improve On: Today's Beauty Lesson Is:

Today I Made An Appointment For: Today's Beauty Lesson Came From:

I WON'T APOLOGIZE FOR MY GLOW UP.

Daily Beauty

Today's Mood: _____   Date: _____   Today's Fragrance: _____

Today's Affirmation:

My Body Feels:

Today My Skin Feels:

Today On My Skin I Used:

Today My Hair Looks And Feels:

Today's Beauty Food:

Today I Am Wearing:

My Style Today Is:

Today My Makeup Look Is:

For My MakeUp Look I Used:

I Internally Took

_____ For

_____ .

Today's Compliment To Myself:

I Will Improve On:

Today I Made An Appointment For:

I Need To Purchase:

I No Longer Need To Purchase:

Today's Beauty Lesson Is:

Today's Beauty Lesson Came From:

Style Tip: If You Suffer From Pain And Blisters From High Heels, Be Sure To Carry Moleskin For Your Feet. Carry Them In Your Purse And Apply To The Areas That Start To Hurt.

MY INSANE WORK ETHIC, MY MORALS, MY UNSTOPPABLE AMBITION AND MY AMAZING BELIEFS IS WHAT MAKES ME BEAUTIFUL.

Daily Beauty

Today's Mood: Date: Today's Fragrance:

Today's Affirmation:

My Body Feels:

Today My Skin Feels:

Today On My Skin I Used:

Today My Hair Looks And Feels:

Today's Beauty Food:

Today I Am Wearing:

My Style Today Is:

Today My Makeup Look Is:

For My MakeUp Look I Used:

I Internally Took

_____For

_____.

Today's Compliment To Myself:

I Will Improve On:

Today I Made An Appointment For:

I Need To Purchase:

I No Longer Need To Purchase:

Today's Beauty Lesson Is:

Today's Beauty Lesson Came From:

Daily Beauty

Today's Mood: Date: Today's Fragrance:

Today's Affirmation:

My Body Feels:

Today My Skin Feels:

Today On My Skin I Used:

Today My Hair Looks And Feels:

Today's Beauty Food:

Today I Am Wearing:

My Style Today Is:

Today My Makeup Look Is:

For My MakeUp Look I Used:

I Internally Took

_____For

_____ .

Today's Compliment To Myself:

I Will Improve On:

Today I Made An Appointment For:

I Need To Purchase:

I No Longer Need To Purchase:

Today's Beauty Lesson Is:

Today's Beauty Lesson Came From:

A List Of Items I Own In My Closet That Have Sentimental Value....

Daily Beauty

Today's Mood: Date: Today's Fragrance:

Today's Affirmation:

My Body Feels:

Today My Skin Feels:

Today On My Skin I Used:

Today My Hair Looks And Feels:

Today's Beauty Food:

Today I Am Wearing:

My Style Today Is:

Today My Makeup Look Is:

For My MakeUp Look I Used:

I Internally Took

_____For

_____ .

Today's Compliment To Myself:

I Will Improve On:

Today I Made An Appointment For:

I Need To Purchase:

I No Longer Need To Purchase:

Today's Beauty Lesson Is:

Today's Beauty Lesson Came From:

Daily Beauty

Today's Mood: Date: Today's Fragrance:

Today's Affirmation:

My Body Feels:

Today My Skin Feels:

Today On My Skin I Used:

Today My Hair Looks And Feels:

Today's Beauty Food:

Today I Am Wearing:

My Style Today Is:

Today My Makeup Look Is:

For My MakeUp Look I Used:

I Internally Took

_____For

_____.

Today's Compliment To Myself:

I Will Improve On:

Today I Made An Appointment For:

I Need To Purchase:

I No Longer Need To Purchase:

Today's Beauty Lesson Is:

Today's Beauty Lesson Came From:

Beauty And Style Notes

Today's Makeup Slay

Daily Beauty

Today's Mood: Date: Today's Fragrance:

Today's Affirmation:

My Body Feels:

Today My Skin Feels:

Today On My Skin I Used:

Today My Hair Looks And Feels:

Today's Beauty Food:

Today I Am Wearing:

My Style Today Is:

Today My Makeup Look Is:

For My MakeUp Look I Used:

I Internally Took

_____For

_____.

Today's Compliment To Myself:

I Will Improve On:

Today I Made An Appointment For:

I Need To Purchase:

I No Longer Need To Purchase:

Today's Beauty Lesson Is:

Today's Beauty Lesson Came From:

Daily Beauty

Today's Mood: Date: Today's Fragrance:

Today's Affirmation:

My Body Feels:

Today My Skin Feels:

Today On My Skin I Used:

Today My Hair Looks And Feels:

Today's Beauty Food:

Today I Am Wearing:

My Style Today Is:

Today My Makeup Look Is:

For My MakeUp Look I Used:

I Internally Took

_____For

_____ .

Today's Compliment To Myself:

I Will Improve On:

Today I Made An Appointment For:

I Need To Purchase:

I No Longer Need To Purchase:

Today's Beauty Lesson Is:

Today's Beauty Lesson Came From:

I'M NOT LIKE THE REST OF THEM.

I'M NOT LIKE THE REST OF THEM.

I'M NOT LIKE THE REST OF THEM.

I'M NOT LIKE THE REST OF THEM.

I'M NOT LIKE THE REST OF THEM.

Daily Beauty

Today's Mood: Date: Today's Fragrance:

Today's Affirmation:

My Body Feels:

Today My Skin Feels:

Today On My Skin I Used:

Today My Hair Looks And Feels:

Today's Beauty Food:

Today I Am Wearing:

My Style Today Is:

Today My Makeup Look Is:

For My MakeUp Look I Used:

I Internally Took

_____For

_____ .

Today's Compliment To Myself:

I Will Improve On:

Today I Made An Appointment For:

I Need To Purchase:

I No Longer Need To Purchase:

Today's Beauty Lesson Is:

Today's Beauty Lesson Came From:

Daily Beauty

Today's Mood: Date: Today's Fragrance:

Today's Affirmation:

My Body Feels:

Today My Skin Feels:

Today On My Skin I Used:

Today My Hair Looks And Feels:

Today's Beauty Food:

Today I Am Wearing:

My Style Today Is:

Today My Makeup Look Is:

For My MakeUp Look I Used:

I Internally Took

_____For

_____ .

Today's Compliment To Myself:

I Will Improve On:

Today I Made An Appointment For:

I Need To Purchase:

I No Longer Need To Purchase:

Today's Beauty Lesson Is:

Today's Beauty Lesson Came From:

Today's Makeup Slay

Daily Beauty

Today's Mood: Date: Today's Fragrance:

Today's Affirmation:

My Body Feels:

Today My Skin Feels:

Today On My Skin I Used:

Today My Hair Looks And Feels:

Today's Beauty Food:

Today I Am Wearing:

My Style Today Is:

Today My Makeup Look Is:

For My MakeUp Look I Used:

I Internally Took

_____For

_____ .

Today's Compliment To Myself:

I Will Improve On:

Today I Made An Appointment For:

I Need To Purchase:

I No Longer Need To Purchase:

Today's Beauty Lesson Is:

Today's Beauty Lesson Came From:

Daily Beauty

Today's Mood: Date: Today's Fragrance:

Today's Affirmation:

My Body Feels:

Today My Skin Feels:

Today On My Skin I Used:

Today My Hair Looks And Feels:

Today's Beauty Food:

Today I Am Wearing:

My Style Today Is:

Today My Makeup Look Is:

For My MakeUp Look I Used:

I Internally Took

_____For

_____ .

Today's Compliment To Myself:

I Will Improve On:

Today I Made An Appointment For:

I Need To Purchase:

I No Longer Need To Purchase:

Today's Beauty Lesson Is:

Today's Beauty Lesson Came From:

Daily Beauty

Today's Mood: Date: Today's Fragrance:

Today's Affirmation:

My Body Feels:

Today My Skin Feels:

Today On My Skin I Used:

Today My Hair Looks And Feels:

Today's Beauty Food:

Today I Am Wearing:

My Style Today Is:

Today My Makeup Look Is:

For My MakeUp Look I Used:

I Internally Took

_____For

_____ .

Today's Compliment To Myself:

I Will Improve On:

Today I Made An Appointment For:

I Need To Purchase:

I No Longer Need To Purchase:

Today's Beauty Lesson Is:

Today's Beauty Lesson Came From:

Daily Beauty

Today's Mood: Date: Today's Fragrance:

Today's Affirmation:

My Body Feels:

Today My Skin Feels:

Today On My Skin I Used:

Today My Hair Looks And Feels:

Today's Beauty Food:

Today I Am Wearing:

My Style Today Is:

Today My Makeup Look Is:

For My MakeUp Look I Used:

I Internally Took

_____For

_____ .

Today's Compliment To Myself:

I Will Improve On:

Today I Made An Appointment For:

I Need To Purchase:

I No Longer Need To Purchase:

Today's Beauty Lesson Is:

Today's Beauty Lesson Came From:

I AM WONDERFULLY MADE.

Beauty And Style Notes

Today's Makeup Slay

Daily Beauty

Today's Mood: Date: Today's Fragrance:

Today's Affirmation:

My Body Feels:

Today My Skin Feels:

Today On My Skin I Used:

Today My Hair Looks And Feels:

Today's Beauty Food:

Today I Am Wearing:

My Style Today Is:

Today My Makeup Look Is:

For My MakeUp Look I Used:

I Internally Took

_____For

_____.

Today's Compliment To Myself:

I Will Improve On:

Today I Made An Appointment For:

I Need To Purchase:

I No Longer Need To Purchase:

Today's Beauty Lesson Is:

Today's Beauty Lesson Came From:

Today's Makeup And Beauty Products

Beauty And Style Notes

WINNING IN MY SKIN.

Made in the USA
Columbia, SC
27 October 2017